Trip of a L

A play

Bill Cashmore and Andy Powrie

Samuel French—London
New York-Toronto-Hollywood

Please see page iv for further copyright information

TRIP OF A LIFETIME

First presented at the Southwold Summer Theatre on 18th August 2000 with the following cast:

Sheila Pollard	Jill Freud
Norman Pollard	Stephen Hancock
Barry Pollard	Bill Cashmore

Directed by Andy Powrie

CHARACTERS

Barry Pollard, 39
Norman Pollard, his father, late 60s
Sheila Pollard, his mother, late 60s

The action of the play takes place on an empty stage, using three chairs or stools to make the settings: Gatwick Airport, an aeroplane, Paris, Frankfurt, Turkey, Egypt, Hawaii, Rio de Janeiro, the Wild West, New York and a cruise liner

Time — the present

TRIP OF A LIFETIME

The play is performed on an empty stage, using three chairs or high stools and a great deal of imagination

SCENE 1

Gatwick

When the play begins, the three chairs are set on the stage

The sounds of a busy airport. We hear an announcement

Tannoy (*voice-over*) Passengers for flight BA four-six-six to Paris, please go to Gate Three. (*Haltingly*) *Les passengers pour BA quatre-six-six à Paris, allez à la porte numero trois, s'il vous plait.*

Barry enters carrying one item of baggage. He puts the item down and looks at his watch

Barry Come on, Dad!

Norman enters. He is carrying a map and scrutinizing it

Oh, for goodness' sake. Over here!

Norman looks up, then returns his attention to the map and walks over to Barry

Barry What are you doing with that?

Norman I thought I'd buy a map.

Barry A map of what?

Norman The area.

Barry (*getting more annoyed*) Which area?

Norman The general location.

Barry Let me see. (*He snatches the map from Norman and looks at it*) Right. We're going on a round the world trip so you've bought a map.

Norman Yes.

Barry Of Gatwick airport.

Norman It's a big place.

Barry It's a waste of money.

Norman It's my money.

We hear the tannoy again

Tannoy (*voice-over*) This is the final call for passengers travelling on BA four-six-six to Paris. Please make your way to Gate Three immediately. *C'est le dernier,* um, call *pour BA quatre-six-six a Paris. Allez à la porte numero trois immediatement.*

Barry Where's Mum?

Norman She went to get some sun stuff.

Barry I told her she'd be able to get it once we're there.

Norman But not from Boots. You know what your mother's like about Boots.

Barry It's ridiculous. It's all the same stuff. And if she doesn't hurry up we're going to miss the plane.

Norman Ah, here she is.

Sheila enters. She is carrying a large W H Smith bag

Sheila Oh, what a palaver!

Norman Did you get the sun lotion?

Sheila Oh, bugger.

Barry You didn't get it?

Sheila No, but I got the new Joanna Trollope and some magazines. For the flight. (*She produces a big pile of magazines—including FHM—from the bag*)

Barry We're going to Paris. It only takes an hour and a quarter.

Sheila There are other flights.

Norman (*looking at FHM magazine*) "Ferhum". What on earth is this? It looks pornographic.

Sheila FHM. It's for Barry. He needs something a bit more racy.

Barry Why?

Sheila To take you out of yourself. You've been cooping yourself up since … Well, we don't need to go back over all that.

Barry I hardly think a ridiculous lad's magazine is the answer to my problems.

Norman Come on you two. They're starting to board.

Sheila Try it anyway, Barry. For me.

Barry scowls. They pick up their things

We hear the tannoy again

Tannoy (*voice-over*) Flight four-six-six is ready to board. Passengers in rows twenty-five to forty-five first, please. *BA quatre-six-six est* prepare, er, *et les passengers avec*. Oh. *Allez vite.*

They all exit

SCENE 2

Taking off

Barry, Sheila and Norman return without any luggage; Norman carries FHM magazine

They set the three chairs next to each other in a row and sit, Barry in the middle. Norman studies FHM magazine intently

Barry All right, Mum?

Sheila I suddenly feel nervous.

Norman It's her first time in an aeroplane, Barry. Be sensitive.

Barry I am. That's why I'm talking to her.

Sheila I'm fine.

Barry Safest form of travel, Mum. Statistically, you could fly every day for five hundred years before you were in a fatal crash.

Sheila Isn't that interesting.

Captain (*voice-over*) Good-morning ladies and gentlemen. This is Captain Roland. I hope you enjoy your flight with us today. Conditions in Paris are good: a bit of light cloud and a temperature of fifteen degrees. We're just waiting for permission to push back and hopefully we should be on our way. Please do take time to read the safety cards provided and watch the safety demonstration. Thank you.

Norman Remember I did four years in the RAF, dear.

Sheila I know. And you pulled through.

Norman Yes.

Barry He was a cook.

Norman A chef.

Barry Chef, cook, whatever.

Sheila An army marches on its stomach.

Norman Ah, we're moving.

Sheila Should we be going backwards?

Norman Don't worry. We're being pushed away from the buildings.

Sheila Pushed??

Barry They have to do this before we can taxi onto the runway.

Sheila Ah.

We hear a binging noise

Captain (*voice-over*) Cabin crew doors to automatic.

Sheila What does that mean?

Norman and Barry make to answer but stop: neither actually knows

We hear the engines spool up and begin to scream. Sheila holds hands with Barry. Barry holds hands with Norman. They are all forced back into their chairs; we see that Sheila and Norman are thrilled, Barry is absolutely terrified. They all tip back slightly in their chairs as the plane takes off. Then they level off. The sound abates

Sheila What fun!

Barry undoes his seatbelt (mimed)

Barry Excuse me. (*He climbs over Norman and rushes to the back of the cabin to be ill*)

   Barry exits

Sheila Oh dear. Poor Barry.
Norman (*still engrossed in FHM*) He'll be OK.
Sheila He gets so stewed up.
Norman Silly.
Sheila Still. Paris. The city of romance.
Norman Oh yes.
Sheila Norman.
Norman What?
Sheila Look at me.
Norman What?
Sheila Happy anniversary.
Norman Ah, yes. Well remembered. Happy anniversary.

Scene 3

Paris

Typical French folk music plays; this fades as the scene begins

Barry enters with a guidebook

The trio arrange the chairs as if they are in a Parisian café

Sheila exits

Barry and Norman sit

Norman Good table. A perfect view.
Barry It's nine hundred and eighty-five feet high.
Norman Is that taller than the Blackpool Tower?
Barry It doesn't say.
Norman When was it built?
Barry 1889.
Norman Who by?
Barry Why by? Who by? By Gustave Eiffel of course. Why do you think they call it the Eiffel Tower?
Norman It doesn't necessarily follow. Who built the Blackpool Tower? Gustave Blackpool?
Barry Don't be ridiculous.
Norman Have you ordered tea?
Barry Not yet. The waitress is busy.
Norman No, she's not. She's biting her nails over there. (*He waves*) *Excusez-moi, garçon!* Do you want tea, Barry?
Barry Er, yes, tea.
Norman Two teas, please. Teas. English breakfast tea.
Barry She doesn't speak English, Dad.
Norman Typical of the French that.
Barry (*loudly*) Two teas, please. (*He mimes pouring tea*) *Deux* teas, *s'il vous plait*. What is the French for tea?
Norman I don't know. Ask your mother.
Barry She's gone to buy some postcards.
Norman *Thé*. Try that.
Barry (*turning back to the waitress*) *Deux thé* ... Oh, she's gone now.
Norman Honestly.

Sheila enters carrying a plastic shopping bag. She is feeling rather jolly

Sheila *Bon apres-midi, mes hommes.*
Barry Mum.

Sheila *Comment allez-vous?*

Norman (*trying to join in*) *Tres bien, merci.* Although we're having awful trouble getting any tea.

Sheila I don't want tea. I'd prefer coffee — this is Paris.

Norman You never drink coffee. It makes you go.

Barry I knew it wouldn't be long before we got round to the subject of the lavatory.

Sheila We all do it, Barry.

Barry Yes, but we don't discuss it at the tea table. It's ridiculous.

Norman Did you get the postcards, Sheila?

Sheila Oh, bugger.

Norman I was hoping to send one to Gerald Warsop. To thank him for those delphiniums.

Barry There'll be plenty of time for postcards. Where's that waitress?

Sheila (*producing a silk scarf from the bag*) But I did buy this lovely scarf. What do you think?

Norman Lovely. How much?

Sheila You always think of the cost, Norman. It spoils things.

Barry I'm paying for the holiday, Dad. Don't forget.

Sheila To celebrate our fiftieth wedding anniversary, Norman.

Norman So you keep reminding me.

Barry (*getting up*) I'm going to get some tea.

Sheila (*also getting up*) Oh, forget the tea. Let's go up the tower while it's so lovely.

Norman (*following suit*) Good idea. After all, we'll be in Germany this time tomorrow.

Barry But it's tea time.

Sheila Don't be such a stick-in-the mud, Barry. That's your trouble. Too stuck in your ways.

Norman It's probably why Laura left you.

Barry Thanks Dad.

Sheila You've got to move on. I'm determined to find you a nice young lady on this holiday. If it's the last thing I do.

Norman Your mother has spoken.

Barry It's ridiculous.

SCENE 4

Frankfurt

German oompah music plays, fading as the scene begins

The chairs are moved ready for Scene 5 — giving the impression of a sauna

Barry, Norman and Sheila take up a position at the front of the stage, staring up distractedly

Sheila I'm not convinced Frankfurt was a good idea.
Norman No.

They look bored

Barry Meant an extra flight.
Sheila And you being sick again.
Barry Mum.
Norman I'll be glad when we get to Turkey.

SCENE 5

Turkey

Turkish music plays, fading as the scene begins

Norman exits

Barry and Sheila collect towels from off stage and wrap them around themselves (over their clothes) and sit, as if in a mixed sauna. It is very hot

Sheila Seems funny sitting in a sauna with you.

Barry Now who's being staid.
Sheila I thought they'd have separate ones. Mens' and ladies'.
Barry It's different in Turkey. They're more laid-back.
Sheila Bit too laid-back for my liking.
Barry I'm going to have a massage later.
Sheila Are you?
Barry All over. With oils.
Sheila Not for me. I don't like to be touched by strangers. Good for you though, Barry.
Barry Why?
Sheila Might meet a young lady.
Barry Don't be ridiculous.
Sheila Never know.

Norman enters. He is not wearing a towel

Norman Ah, here you are.
Sheila Norman!
Barry Dad!
Norman What?
Sheila Put a towel on.
Norman Why?
Barry Because people are watching.
Norman Let them.
Sheila You should not be exposing yourself at your time of life.
Norman I'm on holiday.
Barry (*appealingly*) Dad.
Norman I want to get the full benefit to my pores. *Particularly* at my time of life.
Barry Oh, God.
Norman You should try it, Sheila. It's very liberating.
Sheila I'm sure.

There is silence for a moment as they all try to enjoy the heat

Sheila (*ripping off her towel*) Oh, to hell with it. When am I next going to be in a Turkish sauna?

Barry Mum!

Norman She's got the idea.

Barry I can't believe this is happening.

Sheila Oh, it's lovely, Norman.

Norman You see.

Sheila You want to try it, Barry. It really makes you feel different.

Barry I'm certainly not sitting in the buff in front of you two.

Norman Why not?

Sheila I've seen it all before.

Barry But not for at least thirty years.

Norman It's healthy.

Barry No.

Sheila I don't know, Barry, no wonder Laura ——

Barry Please stop saying that. My failed marriage had nothing to do with me taking my clothes off.

Norman Probably the cause of the problem.

Barry Dad.

Sheila It hardly lasted five minutes.

Barry Four years and three months, actually.

Sheila You have to work at these things, Barry.

Norman Bit of staying power.

Sheila Your father and I have been married for fifty years.

Barry I know. And we're celebrating that very fact.

Sheila In our day, you stuck at it. You didn't give up at the drop of a hat.

Barry I can't believe this.

Norman Your mother's right.

Barry I am thirty-nine years old and I am being lectured on marital relations in a Turkish sauna by my aged and nude parents.

Sheila We may be aged and nude but you'd do well to heed our advice.

Norman After all, you've got your whole life in front of you. Not like us.

Barry I'm going to have my massage.

Sheila All right. But you can't put your life on hold, Barry.

Barry I'm not. (*He gets up to leave and then suddenly rips his towel off*) There. Satisfied?

Barry exits with his towel

A pause

Sheila Not as I remembered him.

SCENE 6

Egypt

Egyptian music plays; we also hear the sounds of a market. The music and sounds fade as the scene begins

Barry enters

Sheila exits with her towel and returns without it

Barry and Norman arrange the chairs in a line. The trio stands on the chairs; they are riding on camels

Sheila Look, Norman. They've got some lovely pots at that stall.
Norman I can't look. I'm worried this camel is going to do something extraordinary.
Barry The man's leading it, Dad. You're safe.
Norman I don't feel safe.
Sheila And those beads. Beautiful colours.
Barry Lucky you can't get down, Mum. You'd be buying the place up.
Norman Couldn't agree more, Barry.
Sheila It's fun on a camel. Reminds me of our first car, Norman.
Norman The Austin.
Sheila No, the Morris Minor.
Norman That wasn't our first car. I bought the Austin first. From that chap in Hinckley.
Sheila No. That was later.
Barry Does it matter?

Sheila Yes. The Austin was quite smooth. Nothing like a camel.
Norman Whereas the Morris was terribly bumpy.
Barry Like a camel?
Sheila Yes.

Music plays, suggesting a romantic evening

The trio dismounts from the camels

   Barry exits

Norman and Sheila stand in front of the chairs

It is night-time. Norman and Sheila are standing in front of the pyramids, arm in arm

Sheila Why a pyramid?
Norman What do you mean?
Sheila It's such an awkward shape. Why not just build a big, square tomb?
Norman Wouldn't be so impressive.
Sheila No. Suppose not.

A pause

Norman Are you enjoying your trip of a lifetime, dear?
Sheila Oh yes. Do you think Barry is?
Norman I think so. More or less.
Sheila I know he's bought the holiday for us but I do want it to be nice for him as well.
Norman I'm sure it is.
Sheila Wish he wasn't so ill on the aeroplanes.
Norman Can't be helped. The RAF cured me of all travel sickness.
Sheila I'd never been on a plane before but I don't seem to suffer.
Norman You're just very clever.

They look into each other's eyes and smile. They are about to kiss

Barry enters

Barry It's fantastic round the other side. With the moonlight.

Sheila Yes. We must come and see.

Barry Do you know, there are over two hundred and fifty thousand stones in this pyramid.

Sheila That's interesting.

Barry And it took nearly twenty years to complete.

Norman You needn't go to so much trouble when I pop my clogs, Barry.

Barry No. I'll only use one hundred thousand stones.

They laugh

Sheila Are you enjoying your holiday, Barry?

Barry Yes. Why?

Sheila Just wondered.

Barry Anyway, it's not my holiday. It's yours.

Sheila But we want you to enjoy it, Barry.

Norman Not just seem like a chore.

Barry It's not a chore. Don't worry.

Sheila You miss Laura, don't you?

Barry Oh, Mum.

Sheila But you do, don't you? Don't worry, we're not going to give you another lecture.

Norman Or take our clothes off.

Barry Good. Yes, I miss her. I … Yes. She'd love this. (*Pause*) Exotic. (*Pause*) I think she felt I cramped her style. Hemmed her in. I didn't mean to. (*Pause*) I'll get over it. In time.

Sheila Course you will.

A pause

Norman Your mother and I never really liked her, actually.

Sheila Norman.

Norman Don't know if that helps.

Barry (*wryly*) Yes Dad. It really helps.

Sheila Come on. Let's go and see the other side.

Norman Yes. The bus goes back in fifteen minutes so we'd better get our skates on.

Sheila The bus driver puts me in mind of that postman we used to have.

Norman Old Brian?

Sheila No, not old Brian. The one after him. When we lived in Wellin Close.

Norman Oh, him.

Norman and Sheila exit, followed by Barry shaking his head

Scene 7

Hawaii

We hear slide guitar and we are in Hawaii

The trio enters. They each wear a garland around their necks, sporting them rather self-consciously

They arrange the three chairs in a row one behind the other, facing R, and sit. They are on a bus

The music cross-fades into a voice-over

Tourist Guide (*voice-over; rather patronizing*) Welcome to all our new friends. Temperature today is a comfortable eighty-five degrees. As you can see, the physical beauty of Hawaii is unparalleled. If you look to your right ——

They all look us

—— you'll see majestic mountains which were created millions of years ago by volcanic activity that thrust these islands three miles from the ocean floor. On your left ——

They all look towards the audience

— the palm-fringed ocean. Truly this is a Pacific paradise. But there are no strangers in paradise. The most beautiful part of Hawaii is the genuine warmth of our people. We call it the spirit of Aloha. Now sit back and enjoy the air-conditioned comfort of this coach as we head for Waikiki beach.

Norman I'll tell you what, Barry.

Barry What?

Norman If that Elvis Presley film's anything to go by you should find the girls here very friendly.

Barry Oh can we change the record?

Sheila (*in a loud whisper*) Norman! *Norman!*

Norman What?

Sheila You see the woman two rows ahead? With the hair.

Norman (*looking*) Er … yes.

Sheila Is it Stephanie Longshore's sister?

Norman I can see what you mean. But isn't she in a home?

Sheila No, that's her mother.

Norman Ah.

Sheila I wonder where she got that hair colour. I'm bored with mine.

Norman Yours is lovely; what's wrong with it?

Sheila I just fancy a change.

Norman You could have dreadlocks!

Sheila (*laughing*) You could too! That would shake up the allotment committee. Yo! Respec'.

Sheila and Norman make hip "street" gestures, accompanied with much yo-ing. Barry is horrified

Barry Excuse me! Oi! Have either of you noticed that we are travelling through some of the most extraordinary flora and fauna in the world? Does this volcano hold no interest for you?

Sheila Sorry, darling. We were having fun.

Norman That told us.

Sheila Behave, Daddy.

Norman and Sheila giggle and try not to

Barry Oh, I give up.
Norman Loosen up, Barry. Once you've seen one volcano you've seen them all.
Barry Oh, fine. Right. So next time I consider taking you on a round the world trip I'll save my money, shall I?
Sheila We really appreciate it Barry. We're so grateful. We're just enjoying ourselves.
Norman You should take a leaf from our book.
Sheila (*warningly*) Norman.
Norman And let's face it, no-one likes a bore.
Barry I beg your pardon.
Norman Well, what do all those Lonely Hearts columns say? "Wanted: person with Good Sense Of Humour."
Barry Just exactly what are you saying?
Norman Nothing.
Barry You are! You're saying I'm boring.
Sheila Of course he isn't, Barry.
Barry He is! He's saying that you two have been together for fifty years because you've got a sense of humour, and the clear implication is that my marriage fell apart because I'm boring.
Sheila He didn't say that, and he didn't mean that, did you, Norman?
Norman (*hesitantly*) Well …
Barry See! He did! He said I'm boring and I've got no sense of humour. I'm not boring!
Sheila Of course you're not.
Barry And I've got a perfectly well developed sense of humour.

Norman raises an eyebrow

Sheila We know.
Barry I know lots of jokes.
Sheila Yes. Tell us a joke Barry.
Norman Oh yes, go on, Max Miller.

Barry I will!
Sheila Oh good.
Barry (*thinking*) Right.

There is a pause. Barry trawls his memory

Norman The anticipation's killing me.
Sheila Norman!
Barry Right. Now don't interrupt. OK. Ready?

Norman and Sheila nod

A man walks into a bar and goes "Ouch". (*Pause. Mistiming the punchline horribly*) You see it was an iron bar.

There is an uncomfortable pause

Sheila Barry, it doesn't matter. No-one cares whether you can tell jokes or not. There's more to nice personality than making people laugh.
Barry No. Dad's right.
Sheila (*fiercely*) No, he isn't!
Norman No, no I'm not.
Barry Don't try to make it better. You're right and it's about time I faced it. Laura walked out on me and moved in with my best friend because I bored both of them to tears. I've been a teacher for too long.
Sheila You're not a teacher, you're a Deputy Head.
Barry Exactly. I spend my waking hours telling people not to run in the corridors, shut up, sit still, stop laughing, stop talking ... I've become a total killjoy.
Sheila (*half-heartedly*) No.
Norman Not totally.

Sheila bashes Norman on the back

There is a pause

Norman is fed up with the turn of events. He starts whistling "Blue Hawaii" or something similar

Barry Right!
Sheila Sorry?
Barry I'm not going to be boring!
Norman Good.
Sheila Don't feel you need to tell us any more jokes, dear.
Barry I'm going to get a life. And sod Laura.
Norman Good for you. I told you I never liked her. Funny eyes.
Barry Dad! Leave it.
Sheila You have some fun, Barry. You need it.
Barry I do. You're right. OK. Today's going to be the first day of the rest of my life. Let's boogie!

Norman looks as if Barry has gone barmy, but is nonetheless relieved

Barry Surf's up dudes!
Sheila Let's ride the white horses!

The "Hawaii Five-O" music plays and all three mime paddling in sync on both sides of the seats. They get up together and exit still paddling their boat

The music cross-fades from the "Hawaii Five-O" theme back to steel guitars

Norman and Sheila enter with large and elaborate cocktails. They sit around an imaginary small table

Norman No wonder the lads round here are so large. They do eat well.
Sheila That was a gorgeous meal.

Norman absent-mindedly puts his hand on Sheila's. They are unselfconscious, they are so obviously besotted with each other

Norman Nice to get some time to ourselves.
Sheila Umm. (*Pause*) I'm a bit worried about Barry.
Norman Forget Barry. There's nothing to worry about. At least he learnt something about himself today.
Sheila But he's not boring!
Norman He's not the life and soul of the party either!
Sheila (*reluctantly*) Perhaps not. Is it our fault?
Norman We can't live his life for him. He's made his own choices and we've always been there for him. But he's not like us. Are you sure they didn't swap babies at the hospital?
Sheila (*laughing*) Norman!
Norman Well, you know what I mean. When he was little he wouldn't play cricket with me, he always cried until I let him do his sums.

Barry enters surreptitiously behind his parents, wearing a grass skirt. He moves forward as if intending to surprise them

Sheila Barry loved his sums. He always did well at maths. Top of the class.
Norman I was convinced he would end up an eminent mathematician.

Barry, hearing his parents talking about him, stops and hides in the shadows, listening

Sheila Well, he was good enough to teach maths at junior school, but he was never an original thinker.
Norman To be fair he never got into trouble.
Sheila No, he was very well behaved.

Pause

Norman I wasn't — how should I put it? — (*his tone contradicts his words*) disappointed in him.
Sheila No. Not at all. I was pleased that he went to teacher training college and walked straight into a job.

Norman I wish he'd left home though. I don't mean it nastily, I just mean I wish he'd discovered a bit about real life. You know, sowed his wild oats, made his mistakes, stuck his head over the parapet.

Sheila Yes, he should have moved away from Leamington.

Norman His friends were all a bit dull.

Sheila Oh God, yes. Do you remember his eighteenth birthday party?

Norman (*laughing*) Oh dear! I read him the riot act about nobody to go into the bedrooms, no smoking, no getting drunk etcetera, etcetera. We went out to Marcia's. And I remember when we arrived back at about midnight ——

Sheila —— Barry and his friend Robin Hugill were sitting waiting for us. "Where have you been till this time?" he said.

Norman And they'd mopped the kitchen, scrubbed the bathroom and hoovered the lounge.

Sheila It was a lot cleaner than I'd left it.

Norman I asked if they'd had a great night. Barry said the attendance was a bit disappointing.

Sheila No girls.

Norman But do you remember? Barry said they'd played some party games and had a debate about community policing.

Sheila No-one got drunk,

Norman Because Barry had hidden the booze I bought. He didn't want to encourage bad behaviour.

Sheila No wonder no-one stayed. Apart from Robin Hugill.

Norman Who was so dull he even made Barry look interesting.

We see that this hurts Barry deeply

There is a pause. Norman and Sheila look lovingly at each other. Barry looks small and fragile

Sheila (*changing the subject; archly*) Darling?

Norman Umm?

Sheila Fancy an early night?

Norman What do you think, temptress?

Sheila (*giggling*) Come on, Tiger ...

They weave off, arm in arm, to their room

Barry steps forward and watches Norman and Sheila leave. He cuts a ridiculous figure in his grass skirt. He takes off his garland, then steps out of the grass skirt.

Barry exits slowly with the garland and grass skirt

Scene 8

Rio

South American music plays; there is a carnival atmosphere

Sheila and Norman dance on animatedly with maracas and whistles. Barry follows. He has a bottle of booze and is drinking liberally

They shout above the music but during the following the music fades as if the carnival is passing on up the street

Sheila Fantastic.
Norman I love it.
Sheila We must go up the mountain this afternoon.
Norman Don't think I'll have the energy.
Sheila How high is Sugar Loaf Mountain?
Norman Don't know. Ask Barry.
Barry How the hell should I know? I'm not a walking encyclopaedia.
Sheila I thought you liked facts, Barry.
Barry Oh, shut up.
Norman Don't talk to your mother like that.
Barry Well. It's ridiculous.
Sheila Are you coming with us this afternoon?
Barry No.
Sheila Don't be sulky.

Barry I'm not being sulky. I've just made other arrangements.
Norman Other arrangements?
Barry Yes.
Sheila Are you wanting to do a bit of sightseeing on your own?
Norman Don't blame you. I expect you could do with a bit of a break from your demanding old folks.

By now the music is in the background

Barry I'm meeting someone.
Sheila Who?
Barry Someone I've met. A girl.
Sheila
          | *(together)* A girl?
Norman|
Barry Yes. A girl.
Sheila Who is she?
Barry Her name is Jimena Fereirra da Silva.
Norman Is she English?
Barry Dad.
Sheila What does she do? Where does she live?
Barry Does it matter?
Norman We don't want you falling in with the wrong crowd.
Sheila You hear horror stories of people on holiday.
Barry I'm thirty-nine years old. I know what I'm doing.
Sheila You said that when you married Laura.
Norman And look what happened to that.
Barry *(becoming loud and angry)* You two are impossible. One minute I'm chastised for not getting — whatever I'm supposed to be getting, and then you tell me I'm boring. And you do that giggling behind your hands. I can't relax. I can't be myself. I'm always having to check I'm saying the right thing or check whether ... Oh, I don't know. It's ridiculous. Ridiculous. Bloody ridiculous.

A pause

Norman Barry.

Sheila Darling.
Norman We haven't heard you swear for twenty years.
Sheila This Latin atmosphere suits you.
Norman It's bringing out the red blood in you.
Sheila Do it again.
Barry What?
Sheila Swear. Go on.
Barry No.

We hear the music getting progressively louder again

Sheila I want you to.
Norman And me.
Barry No.
Norman It would make both of us happy.
Sheila It would.
Barry This is ridiculous.
Sheila Just a little swear word for your ageing mother.
Norman It's our holiday after all.
Barry (*firmly*) No.
Sheila A trip of a lifetime you promised.
Norman Trip of a lifetime.
Sheila Still. It's more important that you maintain your dignity ——
Norman — than make your poor old parents eternally happy.
Barry All right. (*Quietly*) Bloody.
Norman Sorry?
Barry Bloody.
Sheila Again.
Barry Bloody. It's bloody ridiculous.

Slowly they all smirk at each other. It becomes a wonderful shared moment

The music picks up again

> *They beam at each other and dance off energetically, swearing in rhythm*

The music fades

The next morning

> *Sheila and Norman trudge on with their suitcases. They are a little worse for wear*

Norman I've rung his room three times.
Sheila And I got the porter to go up there.
Norman He must have stayed somewhere else last night.
Sheila If he doesn't come soon, we'll miss the bus to the airport.
Norman I hope nothing's happened to him.
Sheila Perhaps we should tell the police.
Norman What can they do?
Sheila (*raising her voice slightly*) I don't know. Alert all cars or something.
Norman Please don't shout, Sheila.
Sheila I'm not shouting.
Norman Or raise your voice in any way.
Sheila (*almost shouting*) I'm not. (*This affects her own fragility*)
Norman I'll speak to the Duty Manager again. You wait here.

> *Norman leaves*

There is a pause. Sheila sits on her suitcase. She looks anxious

> *Barry enters*

Barry Mum.
Sheila Oh, Barry. Where have you been?
Barry I've been on the town. I told you.
Sheila Till this time?
Barry There's no harm.
Sheila Did you meet that girl?
Barry Sort of.
Sheila What do you mean, sort of?
Barry I met her friend.

Sheila Was she ill or something?

Barry No. The barman said she wasn't on duty that night.

Sheila On duty. She was a barmaid?

Barry She worked at the bar. Yes. But not as a barmaid.

Sheila In the kitchens then. Or perhaps …

Barry No, Mum. It turns out — she's — a lady of the night.

Sheila (*realizing*) Oh, I see. And her friend was on duty?

Barry Yes.

An awkward pause. Barry is clearly embarrassed by the whole affair

Sheila Did things work out with the friend?

Barry Of course not. What do you take me for?

Sheila Only checking.

Barry I am not in the habit of becoming involved with ladies of loose morals. I'm from Leamington.

Sheila What have you been doing then?

Barry Nothing much. Just walking. And thinking.

Sheila Rio's a dangerous city. You shouldn't walk about alone at night.

Barry I know.

Sheila Oh, Barry.

Norman enters, a bit puffed out

Norman He'll have to follow on in a cab. It's silly for us … Oh, here you are. I've been searching high and low for you.

Barry Sorry, Dad.

Norman We don't mind you meeting up with some dolly bird but at least let your mother and me know …

Sheila Leave it, Norman.

Norman What?

Sheila Let's just get on the bus.

Norman I don't understand.

Sheila (*heading off*) There's nothing to understand. Come on.

Barry I'll explain later, Dad.

Norman I'd be grateful.

They all leave

SCENE 9

The Wild West

Cowboy music plays, continuing in the background under the scene

Barry, Norman and Sheila enter

Barry sits on the back of a chair as if it is a rodeo horse. Norman and Sheila admire from a distance

Norman Ride 'em cowboy.
Sheila Yee-ha.
Norman You're a natural, Barry.
Sheila What larks.

Barry looks at his parents with loathing

Norman If I was thirty years younger, I'd have a go.
Sheila Do you remember, Mel Duggan used to keep a horse in that yard at the back of his bungalow?
Norman No, that wasn't Mel Duggan. Mel Duggan *lived* in a bungalow but set up that dry cleaning business.
Sheila That wasn't Mel.
Norman I'm sure it was.

Barry's attempts at rodeoing become increasingly less controlled. He tries to get his parents' attention during the following

Sheila That was Roger Tome. He drove a Humber and used to rest his arms on the steering wheel. Like this.

Norman No. That was Mr Skerritt.
Barry Dad.
Norman And it was Mr Skerritt who complained about us making too much noise that Christmas Eve.
Sheila Are you sure?
Norman Yes. Sure as eggs are oeufs.
Barry (*desperately*) Dad.
Sheila Who kept the horse then?
Norman Can't remember. I remember the horse.
Sheila Yes. I sometimes saw it on the verge outside Spar.
Barry (*finally getting their attention*) Mum. Dad.
Norman What Barry?
Sheila Your father and I are talking.
Barry Please turn this machine off.
Sheila Oh.
Norman Why didn't you say?

Norman turns off the rodeo machine

SCENE 10

New York

Sheila exits and returns with a small brown paper bag

Barry and Norman rearrange the chairs into a slight semi-circle

The trio sits

We are in a baseball stadium. We hear the sounds and atmosphere of a large stadium

Announcer (*voice-over; highly energetic*) And welcome to the Yankee stadium, the home of the world-famous New York Yankees. It's going to be one hell of a game today, folks, as the

New York Yankees come face-to-face with the Boston Red Sox.
The players' parade will commence in just a few moments but in
the meantime enjoy some hot dog, enjoy some popcorn and get
yourself down to the world-famous New York Yankee souvenir
stall.

Sheila Is it basketball or baseball?

Barry Baseball.

Sheila I won't understand it.

Norman Of course you will. It's like cricket.

Sheila I don't understand cricket.

Norman You do.

Sheila I don't. They stand about so much.

Norman Why does that stop you understanding it?

Sheila There's nothing to follow.

Barry Did you buy that sun stuff at the hotel, Mum?

Sheila Oh, bugger.

Barry We're going to need it today.

Norman Why didn't you get any?

Sheila I meant to. I bought these cherries instead.

Barry Cherries?

Sheila They had them in the hotel shop. They looked so lovely.

Barry We get complementary fruit in our rooms. What do you want
to go buying more for? It's ridiculous.

Norman (*teasingly*) Bloody ridiculous.

Barry Don't start all that again.

Sheila Oh, Barry, you are being tiresome. Ever since Hawaii,
you've been an absolute misery.

Barry According to you two, I've been an absolute misery since the
day I was born.

Sheila I wouldn't say that.

Norman You were happy once. September 1967 I think it was.

Sheila Or was it August?

Norman and Sheila laugh between themselves. Barry looks miserable

Sheila Anyway, I've got a surprise for you later. That'll cheer you
up.

Barry What?
Sheila Wait and see.

A pause

Norman Do I know what the surprise is?
Sheila Yes.
Norman Do I?
Sheila Yes. I told you this morning.
Norman Of course you did. What was it?
Sheila Oh, Norman. You are hopeless.
Norman But that's why you love me.
Sheila Why?
Norman Because of my charming, forgetful, carefree nature.
Sheila You're a senile old fool, you mean.
Norman If you say so.

Sheila and Norman look at each other with deep affection. Barry finds this a bit sickening

Announcer (*voice-over*) The players are ready to take the field. But before they do, a coupla dedications. Anne-Marie Fitowski is ten today. Happy Birthday from Mom and Pop. Big Brian McEvoy is celebrating his birthday as well. Fifty today. Good on you, Big Bri. And finally a huge welcome to the Yankee Stadium for the very first time, all the way from the mother country, Sheila and Norman Pollard and their son Barry. Barry is four years old and Mom and Pop love him dearly.

We hear a crowd singing "Happy Birthday"

Barry Is that the surprise?
Sheila Yes. The hotel arranged it this morning.
Norman Did he say four years old?
Barry Yes.
Sheila They probably couldn't read my handwriting.
Barry Typical.

Sheila Never mind.
Norman It's the thought that counts.
Barry Did you write that stuff about "love him dearly"?
Sheila Oh no, they must have added that bit.
Barry Thanks.
Sheila But it is true. We do love you. Don't we, Norman?
Norman Er … It goes without saying.
Barry Thanks. (*Making to reciprocate*) And, er, I …

We hear the "Stars and Stripes"

We'd better stand for the national anthem.
Norman Not *the* national anthem.
Barry No.
Sheila But we should show respect.

They stand while the US national anthem plays. It builds in volume

There is an awkward sense of unity between the three

They edge slowly off

SCENE 11

Cruising Home

The "Stars and Stripes" fades into the loud hooting of a ship and a swell of nautical music

During the following voice-over Sheila enters carrying a book. She arranges the three chairs as deckchairs

Tannoy (*voice-over*) At three o'clock on the upper deck we'll have deck quoits and at four-thirty there's Aquasize in the pool with Tony, our fitness instructor. Don't forget: this evening, at eight-thirty, our fancy dress ball in the Grosvenor Ballroom, hosted by Captain Markham.

We hear seagulls and the sound of the ship cutting through the waves; these sounds fade as the scene begins

Sheila takes her place in one of the deckchairs. She takes out her book

   Barry enters and strides past Sheila. He is doing circuits of the ship, walking fast

Barry Fifteen.
Sheila Well done, dear.

   Barry exits

   Norman enters. He is looking a bit peaky. He sits

Sheila Better?
Norman Must be something I ate.
Sheila I expect so. Couldn't be sea-sickness.
Norman I was on a troop ship from North Africa for the best part of three weeks. I hardly think it's sea-sickness.
Sheila Mind you there is a bit of a swell.
Norman Yes, I know.
Sheila We're lurching all over the place.
Norman All right.
Sheila Up and down, up and down.

   Norman rushes off

Sheila Norman?

   Barry enters and walks past Sheila

Barry Sixteen.
Sheila Barry!
Barry (*stopping*) What?
Sheila Have a rest.

Barry (*his looks belying his words*) I'm feeling fine.

Sheila Sit down. Relax.

Barry (*sitting*) Oh, all right. Where's Dad?

Sheila Funny tummy.

Barry (*pleased*) He's seasick!

Sheila Oh no, he ate something.

Barry (*smugly*) Of course.

Sheila We've had a wonderful trip, Barry. Thank you so much. I hope it hasn't been too dull for you.

Barry No. Not at all.

Pause

Sheila Did I see you talking to a girl?

Barry Please Mum! I'm thirty-nine. I do speak to women occasionally.

Sheila Sorry! I just had the impression you were getting on well.

Barry I know her. Sandra Nightingale. We were at teacher training college together.

Sheila That's a coincidence. (*Pause*) Is she … ?

Barry No, she isn't married! She's separated. Now can we drop the subject before you ask the Captain to start reading the banns?

Norman appears, staggering somewhat. He makes it to his deckchair then rushes off again

Barry snorts with barely disguised amusement

Sheila Oh dear. (*Then she laughs*)

Barry Do you think he'll be all right for the Fancy Dress?

Sheila I expect so. Your father has always loved dressing up. But that's another story.

Barry You're a hard act to follow.

Sheila We are?

Barry I know you can't understand how I've failed to sustain any sort of long-term relationship. But that's because you've found it so easy. You've been lucky. To find the love of your life in your teens, marry and live happily ever after. It just doesn't happen to most of us.

Sheila I know. We've been fortunate.

Barry I tried, you know.

Sheila Of course you did.

Barry I thought that Laura was my future. I was very happy with her, and I couldn't imagine a life without her. But when she left I wasn't given any choice. She'd made her mind up. (*Pause*) I never told you exactly how it happened did I?

Sheila We didn't want to pry.

Barry It was Christmas Eve.

Sheila Oh no.

Barry Good timing eh? We'd had Trevor and Christine over for drinks and it was a really nice evening. They went at about two o'clock on Christmas morning and Laura and I sat to have a final drink. She took a deep breath and said "You know there's something wrong don't you?" But I didn't. I thought everything was great. Then she said "I'm sorry but I'm leaving you, Barry." I asked her why and she said she couldn't see a future with me. It didn't matter what I said, she'd decided. (*Pause*) Christmas Day was a bit of a muted affair. People were very supportive. Trevor and Christine. Trevor took a particular interest. We had a lot in common. He'd been seeing Laura for the best part of a year. I'm not sure if it was better or worse that she'd fallen in love with someone else. I suppose it was better. I think it would be worse if she'd just rather be on her own than with me. (*Pause*) Anyway, I don't want to bore you any more with it, but the point I'm making is that I did work at the relationship — I think I did. I tried. But if someone falls out of love with you — it's not your fault. It's no-one's fault. It happens. And it happened to me.

Sheila I know. I'm sorry.

Barry So … Anyway.

Sheila Plenty more … (*she thinks better of saying " fish in the sea"*) no.

Barry No. Thank you.

There is a pause

Sheila (*getting up*) Will we see you at the fancy dress?
Barry Perhaps.
Sheila I'd better go and look after your father. He's such a baby
when he's ill.

Sheila exits

Barry moves the chairs to form a line DS. *This is the ship's rail*

We hear the Mantovani Orchestra playing some stirring love song

*Norman enters, dressed as Cupid, with a bow, arrow and wings
over his normal clothes*

*Sheila enters, with a Maid Marion costume added to her normal
clothes*

*Norman and Sheila dance with each other. The music fades and they
stop dancing*

They are on deck in the moonlight

*Norman exits and returns with a bottle of champagne and three
glasses on a tray*

*Norman pours the champagne and puts the tray down. Norman and
Sheila take a glass each and sip from it. They look out to sea, arms
round each others' waists*

Sheila You look very dashing, Robin.
Norman Robin?
Sheila My merry man.
Norman I'm not Robin Hood! I'm Cupid.
Sheila Oh! Very good.
Norman Robin Hood hasn't got wings.

Sheila Is that what they are?
Norman I don't know why I bother.
Sheila Sssh!
Norman What?
Sheila (*who has seen something*) Don't look round.

Norman immediately does so. Sheila grabs him

Don't look!
Norman I don't know what I'm not supposed to be looking at.
Sheila It's Barry. And the girl he's met,
Norman What that dumpy one with the long hair?
Sheila She's not dumpy. Honestly I dread to think what you say
   about me when I'm not here.
Norman You're not dumpy.
Sheila They're kissing!
Norman (*grimacing*) Do you mind? I've got a delicate constitution.
Sheila Aw. She looks lovely.
Norman (*peering surreptitiously*) Is she in fancy dress?
Sheila I think so. It's difficult to tell with Barry wrapped around her.
Norman We should leave them to it.
Sheila I do hope it works out for him this time.
Norman He's got three more days before we reach Southampton.
   I'm a bit dubious. He's not a fast mover.

Sheila laughs

Norman Mind you, at least she can't escape. Unless she jumps
   ship!

They both laugh too loudly

Sheila Oh no, we've been spotted.

Barry enters, with a Cyrano de Bergerac costume over his clothes

Barry What are you two doing here?

Norman Nothing.

Barry You are! You're following me around.

Sheila We're not, dear. We were just taking the air. We didn't even know you were here.

Barry Look! I'm trying to have a sensible conversation with an old college friend and you two have to spoil it!

Norman Hang on a minute ...

Sheila Barry calm down. You're being paranoid.

Norman We wouldn't try to spoil anything for you. That's ridiculous.

Sheila Bloody ridiculous.

There is a pause

Barry I'm entitled to a bit of privacy.

Norman No-one's arguing.

Sheila Honestly darling.

Pause

Barry Well ... Look, I'm sorry. I thought you were laughing at me.

Sheila Oh darling. Why would we laugh at you?

Norman Apart from the obvious.

Barry What do you mean?

Norman The hooter. (*He points at Barry's Cyrano nose*)

Barry (*feeling the nose*) Oh right.

Pause

Norman Where's your friend gone?

Barry She's gone to change out of her elephant costume.

Norman tries not to laugh; he snorts and coughs into his handkerchief. Sheila can't help seeing the funny side. Eventually even Barry smiles

Sheila Will you introduce her to us?

Barry Yes. In time, Mum.
Sheila OK.

The ship's hooter blasts. They all lean over the rail

Sheila (*putting her arms round both the men*) My men.
Barry Your merry men.
Norman I'm not Robin Hood!
Barry Who are you then?
Norman Cupid.
Barry God help us.
Norman I made these wings myself.

Barry laughs

Sheila What a journey! Paris, Frankfurt, Istanbul ——
Norman — Egypt, Hawaii, America ——
Barry — Leamington Spa.
Norman I haven't missed home. Not really. But I'll be glad to be back in England.
Sheila Roast beef and Yorkshires.
Barry Ooh, yes.
Norman A decent pint of bitter.
Barry Oh, don't.
Sheila Not living out of a suitcase.
Barry Umm.
Norman Tripe and onions.
Sheila You've never had tripe and onions in your life.
Norman It's never too late.
Barry Absolutely. That's going to be my motto.
Norman Steady on!
Barry Watch this space.
Norman What's he on about?
Sheila The future I think.
Norman I'll drink to that.
Sheila Thank you both.
Norman You're welcome. What for?

Sheila For the trip of a lifetime.

They all lift their glasses and toast

Barry
Norman } (*together*) Trip of a lifetime.
Sheila

Mantovani plays

   They exit slowly, arm in arm

THE END

FURNITURE AND PROPERTY LIST

SCENE 1

On stage: Three chairs or high stools

Off stage: Item of baggage (Barry)
Map (Norman)
WH Smith bag containing magazines including *FHM* (Sheila)

SCENE 2

No additional props

SCENE 3

Off stage: Guidebook (**Barry**)
Plastic shopping bag containing silk scarf (**Sheila**)

SCENE 4

No additional props

SCENE 5

Off stage: Towels (**Barry** and **Sheila**)

SCENE 6

No additional props

Scene 7

Off stage: Hawaiian garlands (**Norman, Sheila, Barry**)
Large, elaborate cocktails (**Norman** and **Sheila**)

Scene 8

Off stage: Maracas and whistles (**Sheila** and **Norman**)
Bottle of booze (**Barry**)

Scene 9

No additional props

Scene 10

Off stage: Small brown paper bag of cherries (**Sheila**)

Scene 11

Off stage: Bow, arrow, wings (**Norman**)
Items to suggest Maid Marion costume (**Sheila**)
Tray. *On it*: bottle of champagne, three glasses (**Norman**)
Items to suggest Cyrano de Bergerac costume (**Barry**)

Personal: **Norman**: handkerchief

LIGHTING PLOT

This play was written to be performed without any lighting changes.

EFFECTS PLOT

Cue 1	When ready *Sounds of a busy airport;* *Tannoy announcement, dialogue as p.1*	(Page 1)
Cue 2	**Norman**: "It's my money." *Tannoy announcement, dialogue as p. 2*	(Page 2)
Cue 3	They pick up their luggage *Tannoy announcement, dialogue as p.3*	(Page 3)
Cue 4	**Sheila**: "Ah." *Binging noise; Captain's announcement,* *dialogue as p.4*	(Page 4)
Cue 5	**Norman** and **Barry** make to answer *Engines spool up and begin to scream*	(Page 4)
Cue 6	Plane levels off *Fade engine sound*	(Page 5)
Cue 7	**Norman**: "Happy anniversary." *Typical French folk music; fade*	(Page 5)
Cue 8	**Barry**: "It's ridiculous." *German oompah music; fade*	(Page 7)
Cue 9	**Norman**: "I'll be glad when we get to Turkey." *Turkish music plays; fade*	(Page 8)
Cue 10	**Sheila:** "Not as I remembered him." *Egyptian music plays; market sounds; fade*	(Page 11)

Cue 11	**Sheila**: "Yes." *Romantic music*	(Page 12)
Cue 12	**Norman** and **Sheila** exit followed by **Barry** *Hawaiian slide guitar music*	(Page 14)
Cue 13	**Norman, Sheila** and **Barry** sit down on the bus *Cross-fade music into Tourist Guide voice-over,* * dialogue as pp. 14-15*	(Page 14)
Cue 14	**Sheila**: "Let's ride the white horses!" *"Hawaii Five-O" music*	(Page 18)
Cue 15	They exit, paddling *Cross-fade "Hawaii Five-O" music* * into steel guitar music*	(Page 18)
Cue 16	**Barry** exits slowly *South American carnival music;* * reduce volume as scene progresses*	(Page 21)
Cue 17	**Barry**: "No." *Bring up volume of music progressively* * under the following*	(Page 23)
Cue 18	They smirk at each other *Bring up music volume to maximum required*	(Page 23)
Cue 19	They exit, dancing *Fade music*	(Page 24)
Cue 20	They exit *Cowboy music, continuing under scene*	(Page 26)
Cue 21	They sit *Cross-fade cowboy music to sounds and* * atmosphere of large stadium; Announcer voice-over,* * dialogue as p. 27-28*	(Page 27)

Cue 22   **Norman**: "If you say so." They look at each other   (Page 29)
            Announcer voice-over; dialogue as p. 29;
               then crowd singing "Happy Birthday"

Cue 23   **Barry**: "And, er, I …"   (Page 30)
            The "Stars and Stripes" plays

Cue 24   **Sheila**: "But we should show respect."   (Page 30)
            Increase volume

Cue 27   They edge slowly off   (Page 30)
            Cross-fade "Stars and Stripes" into loud hooting
               of a ship and swell of nautical music;
               tannoy announcement, dialogue as p. 30;
               seagulls and sound of ship cutting through waves;
               fade

Cue 28   **Barry** moves the chairs to form a line DS   (Page 34)
            Music: the Mantovani Orchestra
               playing a stirring love song

Cue 29   **Sheila**: "OK."   (Page 37)
            Ship's hooter blasts

Cue 30   **All three**: "Trip of a lifetime."   (Page 38)
            Mantovani plays